Triops – a very unusua

by Dr. Helen Pashley
Photos by Lori Adams

Table of Contents

Triops - a very unusual creature
Library of Congress Control Number: 2009928451
ISBN-13: 978-0-9824412-1-3 (hardcover)
ISBN-13: 978-0-9824412-0-6 (softcover)
© 2009 Little Science Books
Published by Little Science Books LLC
Cortlandt Manor, New York

To Dad with love, H.E.P.
To Will and Annona with love, L.A.

For information on other titles visit: www.littlesciencebooks.com

Photographs on pages 16, 18 (eggs) and 23 by Dr. Helen Pashley.

Introduction

Many families have a pet dog or cat at home. Others may have a parrot, an aquarium with fish, or perhaps even a snake or iguana.

Some people keep pet **Triops**. What kind of pet is a Triops? A Triops is a very unusual creature, as you can see in the picture below. Even the name is strange. You call them Triops if there is just one or many. These creatures can be kept in school or at home. They are also studied by scientists in both laboratories and their natural habitat.

Looking at Triops

An adult Triops is about the length of your thumb (5-7centimeters or about 2-2 ¾ inches long). A small greenish brown creature, it can easily fit in your hand. What is the first thing you notice when you look at a Triops from above? A large **carapace** covers its head and the front of the body. Some people call Triops "shield shrimp" because the carapace protects the Triops like armor. It feels hard, but flexible, like your fingernail.

Triops are **invertebrates** because they do not have a backbone or bones inside their body like people do. Instead, they have an **exoskeleton** made of chitin and protein, which covers the whole of the outside of their body. The heart, muscles, and other organs are found inside the exoskeleton.

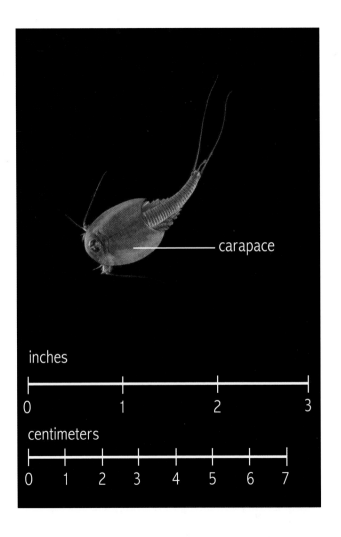

carapace

inches

0   1   2   3

centimeters

0 1 2 3 4 5 6 7

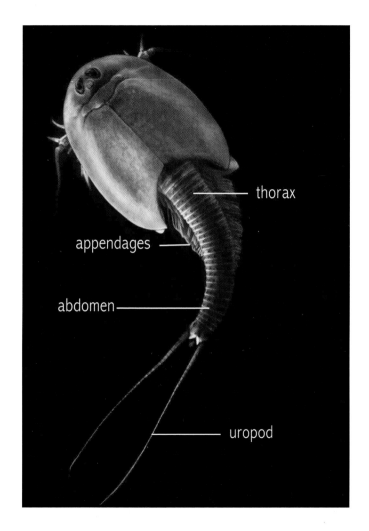

thorax

appendages

abdomen

uropod

The Upper Side of Triops

Behind the carapace you can observe the long **thorax** and **abdomen**. Look for the rings around these parts. There are about 40 altogether, called **segments**. The segments are hard exoskeleton, but they have a thin membrane where they join together. The segments can move over each other so that the Triops can bend its body.

Which part is the thorax and which is the abdomen? Most scientists call the segments that have thin, pink **appendages** the thorax. Those that don't have appendages are part of the abdomen. At the very end of the abdomen are two long tails called **uropods**. The tails act like rudders on a boat to help the Triops turn when it swims.

What else can we observe? Find the brown curving lines on the carapace. The one towards the tail marks where the head ends and the thorax begins.

If you look very carefully by the edge of the carapace you can see an area with little grooves. These are the parts of the Triops that control how much water is in its body.

grooves

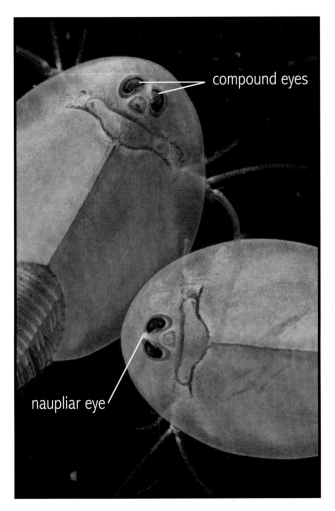

compound eyes

naupliar eye

Eyes

Look carefully at the front of the carapace. Triops have two dark, **compound eyes**. They lie flat on the carapace like tiny black beans. Triops are unusual **crustaceans** because they do not have eyes on stalks like crabs or lobsters. Do Triops see clearly? No. These eyes can only detect food or predators if they are very close.

Why are these animals called Triops? "Triops" means three eyes in Greek! Look more closely and you will see a pale third eye between them. This eye, called a **naupliar eye**, is like a window. It senses if light is shining on the upper or underside of the Triops. This eye is deep inside the body and tells the Triops which way up it is swimming.

trunk appendages —————

The Underside of Triops

What is the first thing you notice when you look at a Triops from underneath? There are lots and lots of pink legs. Triops can have as many as 70 pairs of legs, or **trunk appendages**. They get smaller as you move from head to tail.

Triops are very unusual because as they grow older and larger they get more and more pairs of legs! On each of the first 11 segments there is only one pair of legs. The other segments may have more than one pair of legs like a millipede.

Appendages

Look carefully at the appendages again from the side. Can you see the ones under the carapace that are long, thin and look like legs? They are used for swimming and for collecting food in the water. These longer legs filter out food for the Triops to eat.

Now look at the other appendages. They have a different shape. These appendages are flat and look like red leaves. All together they have a very large surface area which is used for breathing.

What else can you observe underneath a Triops? Can you see the mouth and jaws (or **mandibles**)? They are found behind the yellow square-shaped lip. They are very strong and move from side to side instead of up and down like our jaws.

What you can't see are two pairs of **antennae** like you would observe on a crayfish or lobster. Triops are unusual because their antennae are so small that you need a microscope to see them.

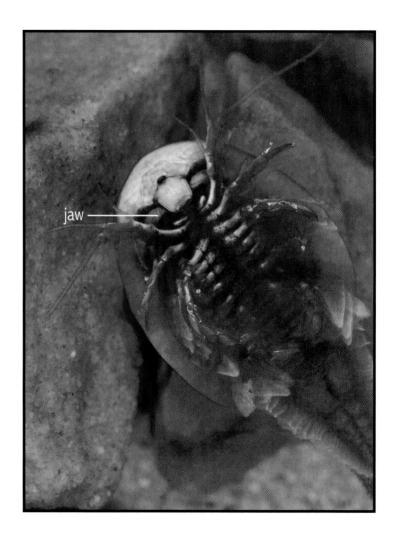

jaw

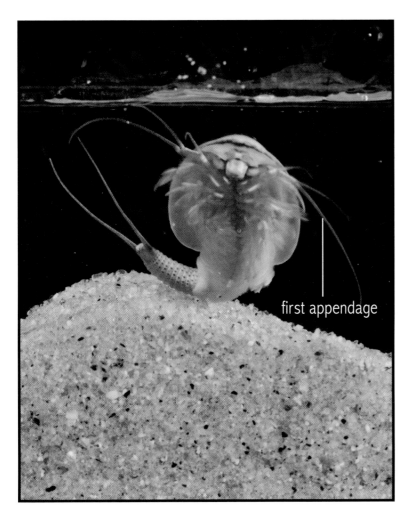

first appendage

If Triops don't have long antennae and their compound eyes don't see clearly, how do they sense the world around them? Look again below the carapace and you will see three long feelers on each side, called **first appendages** (or thoracopods). These special appendages are like a cat's whiskers. They act like the antennae of insects and sense food and chemicals in the water. The first appendages can also test particles to see if they are edible.

How do Triops breathe?

Triops breathe with their appendages, which act like a fish's gills. The appendages are red because they contain **hemoglobin**. Hemoglobin, a chemical containing iron, is also found in our blood. It allows the appendages to get oxygen from the water more easily.

Many other crustaceans have blue-green blood that does not contain hemoglobin.

When the weather is hot and the pools where they live start to dry out, Triops swim upside down. They stay close to the surface where the oxygen levels in the water are higher.

How do Triops move?

Triops move by swimming with their appendages. The appendages move in a waving motion to push them through the still water of a pool. Triops often swim in circles up to the surface and down again like doing somersaults. This helps them collect particles of food that are on the surface and floating lower down in the water.

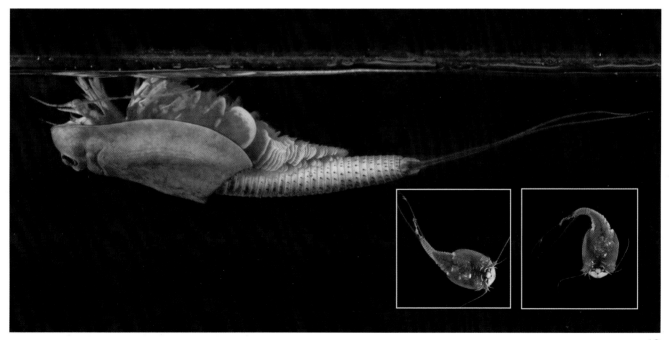

What do Triops eat?

Triops are **omnivores**. This means they eat a mixed diet of plants and animals. Triops will eat algae (small, green water plants), mosquito larvae, tadpoles, fairy shrimp and sometimes other Triops! They may find worms and other little creatures by digging in the mud and sand at the bottom of the pool where they live. Once caught, the powerful jaws or mandibles will rip their prey into pieces and swallow it.

Another way they can feed, is by stirring up sediment with their appendages. After they have collected the food particles, they swim on their backs. They use the inside part of their appendages to push the pieces along a **food groove** to the mouth.

food groove

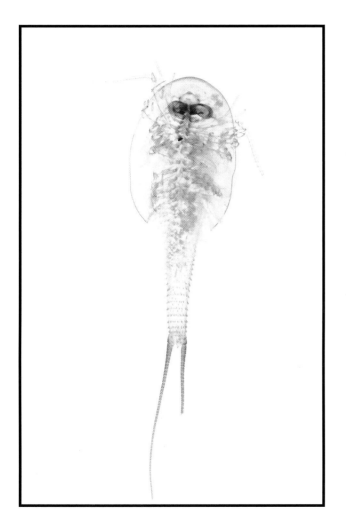

How do Triops grow?

Triops grow incredibly fast. They hatch from tiny eggs the size of poppy seeds and grow to 5 centimeters long (about 2 inches) in a few weeks. Because they have an exoskeleton, they have to **molt** and shed their outside covering to increase in size. Triops may molt 40 times in their short life.

Often you can see their shed exoskeletons in the water. The exoskeleton is a perfect replica of the Triops.

Can you see the strong, brown mandibles in this exoskeleton?

Where do Triops live?

Most Triops live in **vernal** pools. These are temporary, fresh water pools that last for only a short time. In the desert, thunder clouds may produce heavy rain. The rain collects in large and small pools. In the hot sun, the pools may only last a few weeks before they become dried mud. Triops are one of the few animals that have adapted to survive in this type of **habitat**.

Predators and Prey

Wading birds are predators of Triops. Migrating birds stop at the vernal pools where Triops are growing, to drink and feed. They catch and eat Triops swimming in the water.

Triops may also be predators. Small, injured Triops may also be prey for larger Triops.

Egg Laying

Look carefully at the underside of this female Triops. Can you see the **egg pouch** containing eggs? It is found on the eleventh appendage on either side. Sometimes unfertilized white or pink eggs are laid on the bottom of a pool or tank and hatch into **larvae**. This is called **parthenogenesis**. If there are male Triops in the pool, the female will mate before laying eggs. However, some species of Triops are **hermaphrodites** (both male and female). In this case the eggs of both animals are fertilized during mating.

The Life Cycle of Triops

Most Triops do not live very long. After hatching, they only live 50-90 days before they die. Why do they only live such a short time and have such a short **life span**? Triops are adapted to live in temporary pools, which dry up very quickly in **arid** places. The eggs change into **metanauplius larvae** within 24 hours of the first raindrops soaking the dried mud, where they were laid. Can you see how they change? The first larva is about 8 hours old; the second larva is about 15 hours old. They grow to adults in three weeks. Then they lay their own eggs in the sand and mud before dying when the pool dries out.

x40　　x40　　larvae

What animals are Triops related to?

Triops are small, fresh water crustaceans. You may have heard the names of some other crustaceans like crabs, lobsters and crayfish. However, Triops are most closely related to fairy shrimp (sea monkeys) and water fleas. These animals are called **Branchiopods** or "gill-foot" crustaceans because they breathe and move with their legs.

Similar Creatures

Triops may be related to ancient animals like horseshoe crabs and extinct trilobites. Observe how the unusual body shape of this Triops is like these two creatures. Scientists have also found that the development of Triops larvae is similar to the larvae of horseshoe crabs.

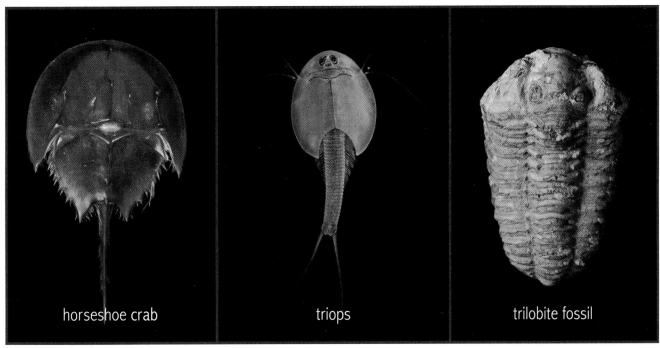

horseshoe crab   triops   trilobite fossil

Living Fossils

Triops are called living fossils. The way they look and live has not changed in over 220 million years. Long before dinosaurs roamed the Earth, the ancestors of these creatures swam in pools in dry, arid places just as they do today. Animals that do not change over time are very well-adapted to live in their particular habitat.

Interesting Facts

Triops lay eggs in the muddy sediments at the bottom of the pools where they live. When the pool dries up, the adult Triops die. However, their eggs dry out and enter a resting stage. This is called **diapause**. The eggs have thick shells which protect them so they can survive the most extreme conditions. The eggs can survive drought or freezing or heating to nearly the boiling point of water or being blown long distances in dust. Diapause may last over 20 years. Scientists have tested the eggs under these conditions. They have observed the eggs hatching once they are put into rainwater again. This survival strategy helps Triops live in dry arid deserts which may be baking hot or freezing cold or dry for many years.

Where in the world do you find Triops?

Triops are found on every continent except Antarctica. They may be found in Africa, Australia, North and South America, the West Indies, Asia (including Japan), throughout Europe, in Arctic pools and several Pacific islands (including the Galapagos and Hawaii).

Triops are found in so many different countries because their eggs may be blown in dust from one place to another, or spread from pool to pool on the legs of frogs and birds. However, their habitat is always a temporary pool, puddle or pond.

Scientists estimate there are over 40,000 different species of crustaceans. There are only 16 species of Tadpole Shrimp. Scientists put Tadpole Shrimp (or Notostraca) into two groups (genera): 6 species are called Triops and 10 species are called Lepidurus.

Triops have many different nicknames. They can be called Shield or Dinosaur Shrimp. In Australia they are called Billabong Bugs. Some giant African species grow to 13-15 centimeters long (5-6 inches). In North America, one kind is called a Long-tailed or Rice Tadpole Shrimp. Scientists use a special name for each species, so everyone around the world knows which kind of tadpole shrimp they are studying. The scientific name for the tadpole shrimp in this book is *Triops longicaudatus*. Longicaudatus means "long tail".

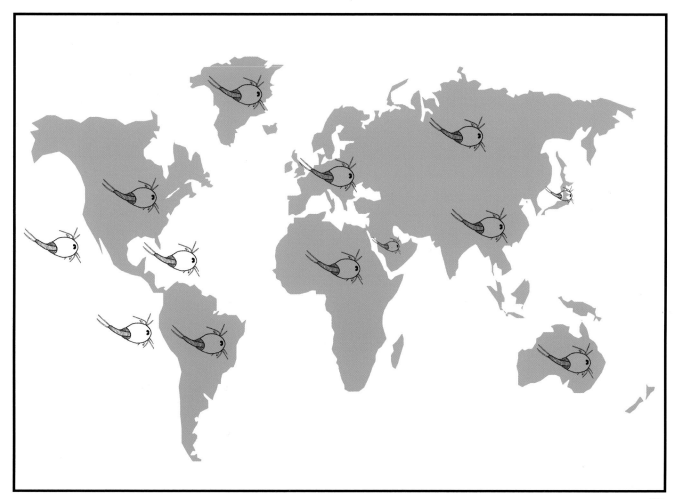

Scientists Study Triops

Scientists hope to understand how diapause works. If they can find out how Triops eggs stop developing, this knowledge may help us in other ways. Scientists think that if they can put astronauts into diapause, the astronauts might be able to travel through the universe for many, many years to visit distant planets without growing older.

Also, if scientists can better understand how to stop cell growth, as in diapause, this might help them control cancer cells.

Some scientists think that Triops may be useful in fighting diseases like Malaria and West Nile Virus. These illnesses are usually found in tropical countries. When a sick person is bitten by a mosquito they carry the disease to the next person they bite. Scientists could drop lots of Triops eggs into the pools where the mosquitoes breed. The Triops could eat the mosquito larvae before they hatch into adults and bite anyone. Triops eggs are very small and survive extreme conditions. It would be easy to spread them from an airplane or carry them from place to place.

Triops can be a nuisance in rice fields where the seedlings are not transplanted by hand. The Triops root up the young plants when they dig for food. Some scientists study how to stop this from happening.

Raising Pet Triops

You can raise pet Triops from eggs, and observe them for yourself. Triops kits and eggs are available from stores that sell educational science toys, or you can order them over the internet. Just search for Triops. Look for a kit that has farm-raised Triops eggs, because these do not destroy Triops natural desert habitat. When you get your eggs, follow the instructions carefully. See if you too can explore the fascinating life of Triops -- a very unusual creature.

Glossary

Abdomen - the rear part of a Triops body with no appendages

Antennae - sense organs on the head of an arthropod, such as an insect or crustacean

Appendages - leg-like or leaf-shaped parts on the thorax

Arid - dry, desert-like

Branchiopods - the class of animals that Triops belong to; branchiopod means "gill-foot"

Carapace - the front part of the exoskeleton that covers the head

Compound eyes - eyes with many lenses

Crustaceans - one group of arthropods including crabs and shrimp

Diapause - temporary stoppage of life processes

Egg pouch - on the 11th appendage in a female where eggs are stored

Exoskeleton - an outside skeleton or shell

First appendages - the appendages that act like antennae

Food groove - an area between the appendages that moves food to the mouth

Habitat - the place where an animal lives

Hemoglobin - the chemical which makes blood red

Hermaphodite - having both male and female parts

Glossary - continued

Invertebrates - animals without backbones

Larva - a stage of the life-cycle after the egg has hatched

Life span - length of life

Mandibles - the mouth parts

Metanauplius larva - a triops larva

Molt - to shed the exoskeleton

Naupliar eye - the third eye of a Triops

Omnivore - a living thing that eats plants and animals

Parthenogenesis - the development of unfertilized eggs

Segment - a ring-shaped part of the exoskeleton

Thorax - part of a Triops body with appendages

Triops - a tadpole shrimp

Trunk appendage - a limb

Uropod - one of two "tails" at the end of the abdomen

Vernal pool - a temporary pool that forms at some times of the year such as spring

Index

A

abdomen 5
antennae 10, 11
appendages 5, 8, 9, 11,
    12, 13, 14, 18
arid places 19, 23
astronauts 26

B

bones 4
Branchiopod 20

C

carapace 4, 5, 6, 7, 9, 11
chitin 4
compound eyes 7, 11
crabs 7

crayfish 10, 20
crustaceans 7, 12, 20, 24

D

deserts 16, 23
diapause 23, 26
dinosaurs 22

E

egg pouch 18
eggs 15, 18, 19, 23, 24,
    26, 27
exoskeleton 4, 5, 15

F

fairy shrimp 14, 20
first appendages 11
food 7, 9, 13, 14

food groove 14
fossil 21

G

grooves 6

H

habitat 3, 16, 19, 23, 24, 25
head 4, 6
hemoglobin 12
hermaphrodites 18
horseshoe crabs 21

I

invertebrates 4

J

jaws 10, 14

Index - continued

ABOUT US

Dr. Helen Pashley has a doctorate in zoology. She is a teacher, as well as a consultant for the popular elementary curriculum in New York called Science 21. She enjoys keeping unusual pets.

Lori Adams has been fascinated with cameras for decades. She is a photographer and teaching artist. She is thrilled to photograph all kinds of living things.

Little Science Books aims to publish high quality books for curious children and budding scientists. We strive to not only give our readers accurate science content, but insights into the nature and process of science. We wish to approach our books from the perspective of science as a human endeavor, and a search for answers to questions. We hope to answer questions that children have, in clear language and illustrated by stunning photographs, realizing that this knowledge will lead to further inquiry.

Little Science Books